I0570105

Little Maestro:
Piano Sheet Music For Beginners & Kids

Sheet Music Pieces Tailored to Provide Essential Practice Material
for Beginning Pianists

Taylor Kent W.

© Copyright 2024 - All rights reserved.

The content contained within this book may not be reproduced, duplicated or transmitted without direct written permission from the author or the publisher.

Under no circumstances will any blame or legal responsibility be held against the publisher, or author, for any damages, reparation, or monetary loss due to the information contained within this book, either directly or indirectly.

Legal Notice:

This book is copyright protected. It is only for personal use. You cannot amend, distribute, sell, use, quote or paraphrase any part, or the content within this book, without the consent of the author or publisher.

Disclaimer Notice:

Please note the information contained within this document is for educational and entertainment purposes only. All effort has been executed to present accurate, up to date, reliable, complete information. No warranties of any kind are declared or implied. Readers acknowledge that the author is not engaged in the rendering of legal, financial, medical or professional advice. The content within this book has been derived from various sources. Please consult a licensed professional before attempting any techniques outlined in this book.

By reading this document, the reader agrees that under no circumstances is the author responsible for any losses, direct or indirect, that are incurred as a result of the use of the information contained within this document, including, but not limited to, errors, omissions, or inaccuracies.

Table of Contents

INTRODUCTION 1

VERY EASY PIECES 3

    HOT CROSS BUNS 4
    FUZZY WUZZY 5
    MARY HAD A LITTLE LAMB 6
    JINGLE BELLS 7
    TWINKLE TWINKLE LITTLE STAR 8
    LONDON BRIDGE 9
    LIGHTLY ROW 10
    WHEN THE SAINTS GO MARCHING IN 11
    BINGO 12
    YANKEE DOODLE 13
    BROTHER JOHN 14
    THIS OLD MAN 15
    LONG, LONG AGO 16
    BILLY BOY 17
    FARMER IN THE DELL 18
    CLEMENTINE 19
    ROW YOUR BOAT 20
    THE MULBERRY BUSH 21
    HAPPY BIRTHDAY 22
    WE WISH YOU A MERRY CHRISTMAS 23
    THE MUFFIN MAN 24
    ALOUETTE 25
    ODE TO JOY 26
    O CHRISTMAS TREE 27
    OH, SUSANNA 28

EASY PIECES 29

    CHOPSTICKS 30
    TEN LITTLE INDIANS 31
    MY BONNIE 32
    CRADLE SONG 33
    DING DONG BELL 34
    ROCK-A-BYE, BABY 35
    WESTMINSTER CHIMES 36
    LITTLE ROBIN RED BREAST 37
    SKIP TO MY LOU 38
    REVEILLE 39
    LE COQ EST MORT 40
    HUSH, LITTLE BABY 41
    LITTLE JACK HORNER 42
    LOVELY EVENING 43
    LAVENDER'S BLUE 44
    WE THREE KINGS 45
    GOOD MORNING, MERRY SUNSHINE 46
    LITTLE BROWN JUG 47
    DIDDLE, DIDDLE DUMPLING 48

Go to Sleep, Lena Darling 49

Jolly Old Saint Nicholas 50

Buffalo Gals 51

Up on the Housetop 52

Papageno-Papegena Duet 53

Rondo alla Turca 54

Heart and Soul 55

Go Round And Round The Village 56

Amazing Grace 57

Deck The Halls 58

Auld Lang Syne 59

Ach Du Lieber Augustin 60

America the Beautiful 61

Away in a Manger 62

All Through the Night 63

Camptown Races 64

The Wayfaring Stranger 65

Home Sweet Home 66

Scarborough Fair 67

Silent Night 68

Danny Boy 69

I Saw Three Ships 70

Bye Baby Bunting 71

Itsy Bitsy Spider 72

Jack and Jill 73

Hickory Dickory Dock 74

INTERMEDIATE PIECES **75**

Va Pensiero 76

Pat-a-Cake 77

Three Craws 78

Down in the Valley 79

Little Buttercup 80

Swan Lake – Pas de Trois 81

Humpty Dumpty 82

Three Blind Mice 83

Blue Bells of Scotland 84

Pop Goes the Weasel 85

God Save the Queen 86

Where Are You Going to, My Pretty Maid? 87

In the Gloaming 88

Swan Lake – Main Theme 89

Aura Lee 90

What Child Is This? 91

Sonata in A Major 93

Daisy Bell 94

Canon in D 95

Good King Wenceslas 96

O Come, All Ye Faithful 97

Hark! The Herald Angels Sing 98

Winter 99

The First Noel 101

Spring 102

Menuet in G Minor 104

Pomp and Circumstance 105

Bourée from Suite in E minor 106

Jesu, Joy of Man's Desiring 107
Gymnopédie No. 1 108
Papageno's Aria No. 1 110
Barcarolle 112
Moonlight Sonata 113

DIFFICULT PIECES **115**

American Patrol 116
Old King Cole 118
Air on the G String 119
Star Spangled Banner 120
Wedding March 122
La Donna è Mobile 123
Too-Ra-Loo-Ra-Loo-Ral 133
Cavalleria Rustica – Intermezzo 135
Pathetique Sonata – 2ND Mov. 137
The Happy Farmer 138
Étude in E Major 139
Träumerei 141
Piano Concerto No. 21 – 2ND Mov. 142

VERY DIFFICULT PIECES **145**

Hello Ma Baby 146
Menuet in G Major 147
Beautiful Dreamer 148
The Entertainer 149
Take Me Out to the Ball Game 150
The Blue Danube 151
I'll See You in my Dreams 153
Down by the Riverside 155
Nocturne in Eb Major 157
Menuet in A Major 159
Eine Kleine Nachtmusik 160
Queen of the Night Aria 162
Für Elise 164
St. Louis Blues 166
O Sole Mio 167
Habenera 169
Solace 170
Barber of Seville – Overture 171
It Had to be You 173

CONCLUSION **175**

Introduction

Welcome to Little Maestro's Piano Sheet Music for Beginners & Kids. Thank you for choosing this book as part of your music education.

Piano Sheet Music for Beginners & Kids is meticulously tailored to provide essential practice material for budding pianists. This collection of sheet music is designed to nurture your skills, boost your confidence, and hone your sheet music reading abilities.

Within the pages of this comprehensive book, you'll discover a rich tapestry of melodies ranging from delightfully easy tunes to more challenging compositions. Each song is carefully curated to offer a progressive learning experience, allowing you to seamlessly transition from playing with one hand to mastering the complexities of two-handed playing. Each piece can be played with one hand while you work your way up to playing with both hands. Whether you're a complete novice or someone seeking to refine existing skills, this book offers a diverse array of musical pieces suited to every level of proficiency.

As you delve into the repertoire contained within these pages, you'll encounter a kaleidoscope of musical genres and styles. From beloved children's songs and soothing lullabies to spirited ragtime rhythms and soulful jazz melodies, there's something to captivate every aspiring pianist's imagination. Explore the timeless beauty of classical compositions by renowned masters such as Mozart and Chopin, and tap into the rich cultural heritage of traditional folk tunes from around the world.

With a keen focus on providing a well-rounded musical education, our book covers a spectrum of musical elements, including different time signatures, keys, and chords. Whether you're navigating the lilting melodies of a waltz or immersing yourself in the intricate harmonies of a sonata, each composition offers a unique learning experience.

If you are looking for something to complement your journey through this book, you may want to check out our first book, *Beginner Piano Lessons for Kids*. Designed as a comprehensive guide to mastering the fundamentals of piano playing, this invaluable resource provides a solid foundation for beginners and children alike. Ranging from learning the keys to reading sheet music, it covers all the essentials you need to become the next virtuoso. By combining the structured lessons of our beginner's guide with the immersive practice material offered in this book of sheet music, you'll embark on a holistic, musical odyssey that fosters growth, creativity, and a lifelong love of music.

As you embark on this musical adventure, let the melodies contained within these pages be your companions, guiding you along the path to pianistic proficiency. Whether you're playing for pleasure or aspiring to reach new heights of musical excellence, *Piano Sheet Music for Beginners & Kids* offers a treasure trove of musical delights waiting to be explored.

Let the journey begin!

2

Very Easy Pieces

Hot Cross Buns

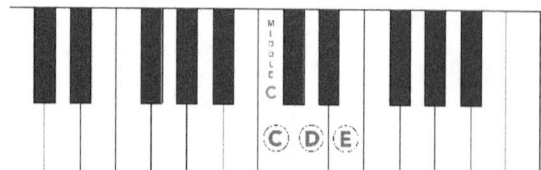  

Fuzzy Wuzzy

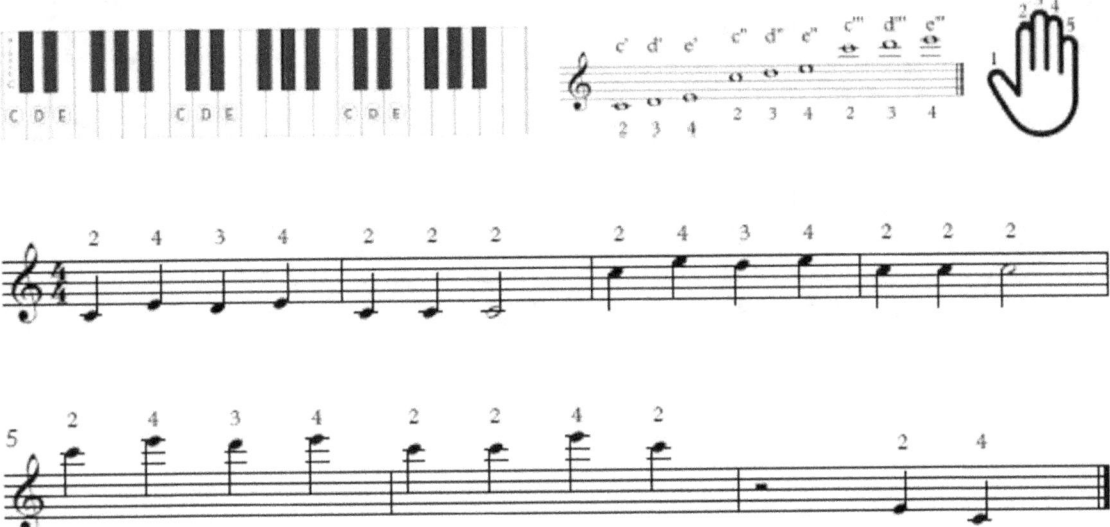

Mary Had a Little Lamb

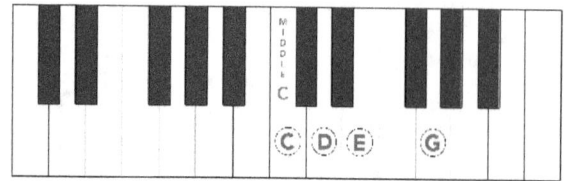 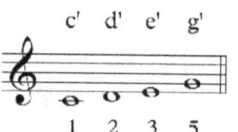 

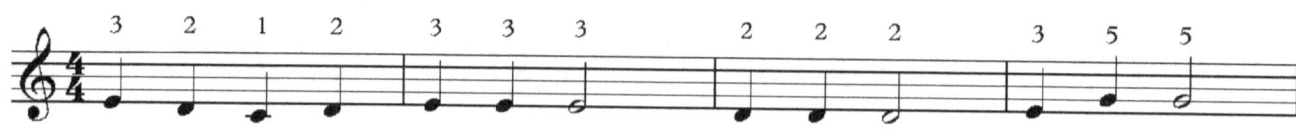

Jingle Bells

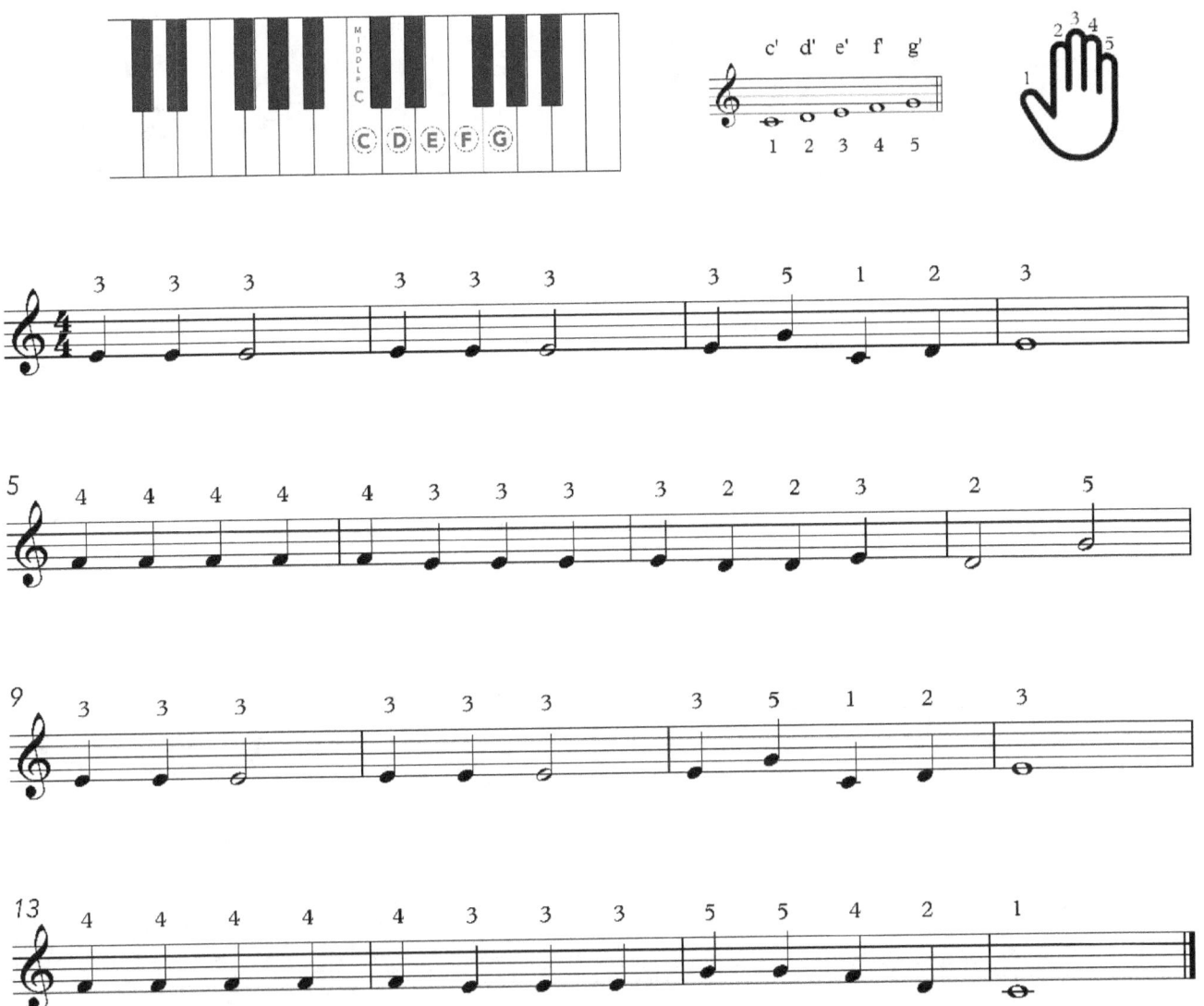

Twinkle Twinkle Little Star

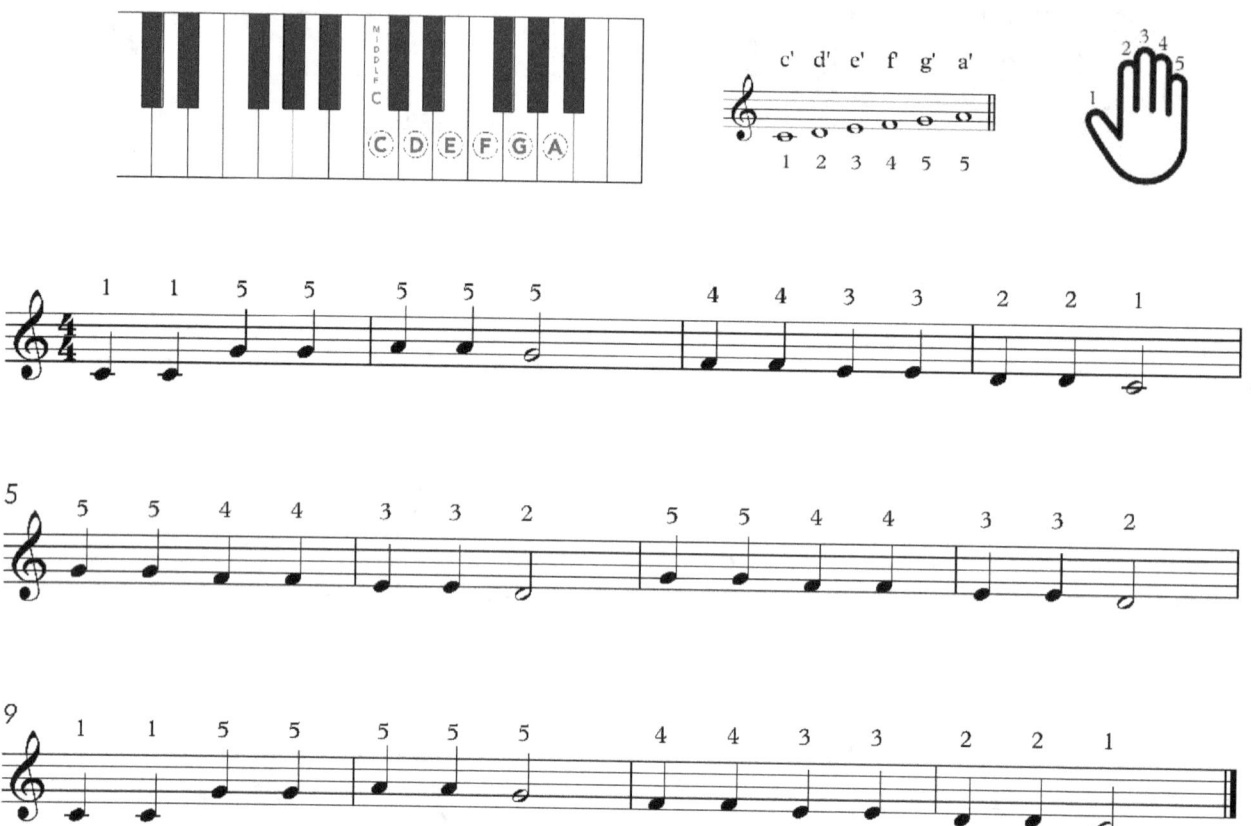

London Bridge

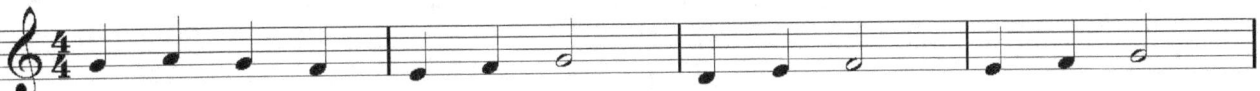

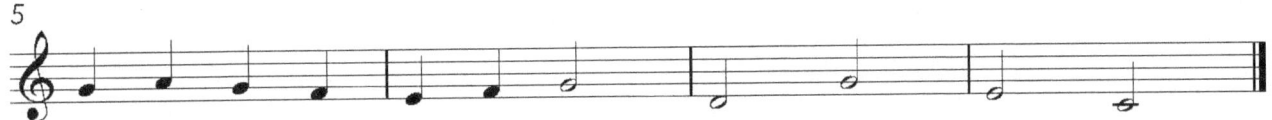

Lightly Row

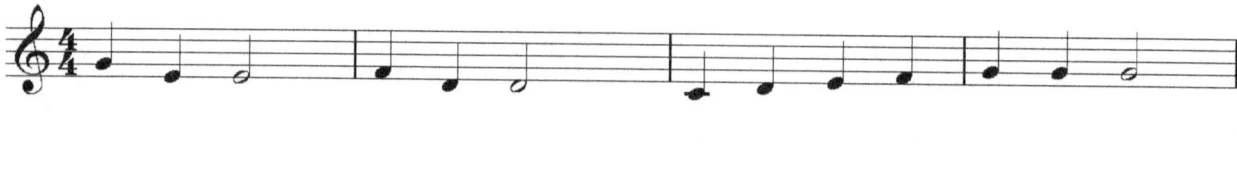

When The Saints Go Marching In

Bingo

Yankee Doodle

Brother John

This Old Man

Long, Long Ago

Billy Boy

Farmer in the Dell

Clementine

Row Your Boat

The Mulberry Bush

Happy Birthday

We Wish You a Merry Christmas

The Muffin Man

Alouette

Ode to Joy

O Christmas Tree

Oh, Susanna

Easy Pieces

Chopsticks

Ten Little Indians

My Bonnie

Andante

Cradle Song

Ding Dong Bell

Rock-a-Bye, Baby

Westminster Chimes

Little Robin Red Breast

Andante

Skip To My Lou

Andante

Reveille

Le Coq Est Mort

Hush, Little Baby

Little Jack Horner

Allegro

Lovely Evening

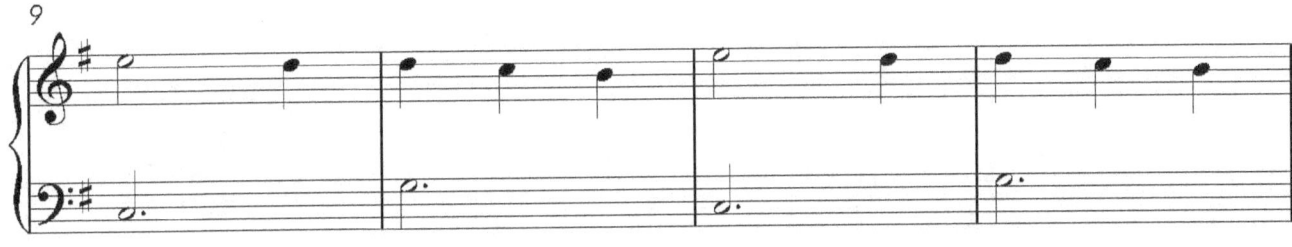

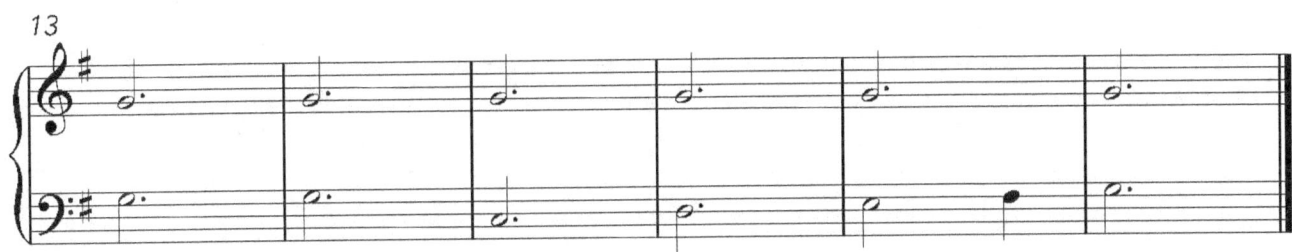

Lavender's Blue

Andante

We Three Kings

Allegro

Good Morning, Merry Sunshine

Allegro

Little Brown Jug

Diddle, Diddle, Dumpling

Go to Sleep, Lena Darling

Jolly Old Saint Nicholas

Allegro

Buffalo Gals

Up on the Housetop

Papageno-Papagena Duet

Mozart

Allegro

Rondo alla Turca

Allegro

Mozart

Heart and Soul

Andante

Go Round And Round The Village

Amazing Grace

Deck The Halls

Auld Lang Syne

Ach Du Lieber Augustin

Andante

America the Beautiful

Away in a Manger

Allegro

All Through the Night

Andante

Camptown Races

The Wayfaring Stranger

Andante

Home Sweet Home

Andante

Scarborough Fair

Silent Night

Danny Boy

I Saw Three Ships

Bye Baby Bunting

Allegro

Itsy Bitsy Spider

Allegro

Jack and Jill

Allegro

Hickory Dickory Dock

Intermediate Pieces

Va Pensiero

Verdi

Pat-a-Cake

Andante

Three Craws

Allegro

Down in the Valley

Little Buttercup

Allegro

Swan Lake - Pas de Trois

Tchaikovsky

Humpty Dumpty

Allegro

Three Blind Mice

Andante

Blue Bells of Scotland

Allegro

Pop Goes the Weasel

Andante

God Save the Queen

Andante

Where Are You Going to, My Pretty Maid?

In the Gloaming

Swan Lake - Main Theme

Tchaikovsky

Andante

Aura Lee

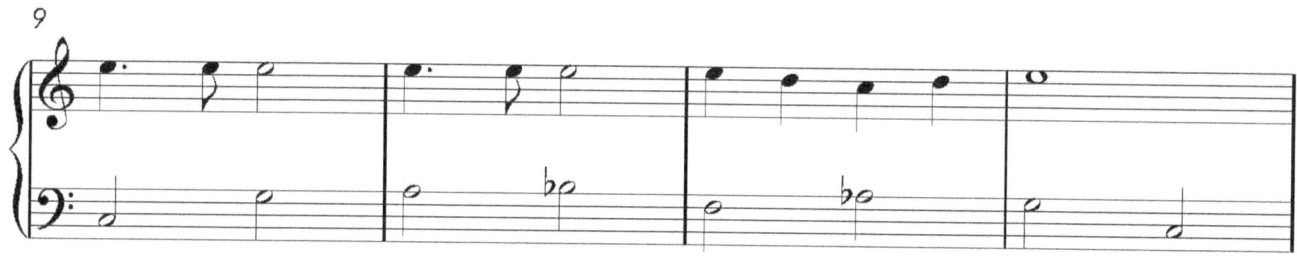

What Child Is This?

Andante

2

17

25

29

Sonata in A Major

Mozart

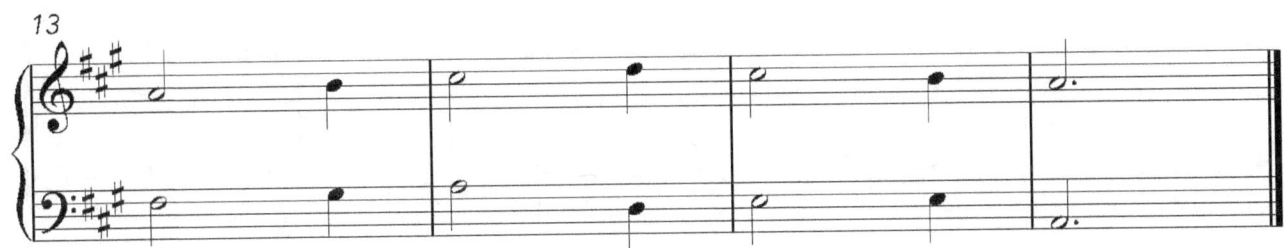

Daisy Bell

Allegro

Canon in D

Pachelbel

Good King Wenceslas

O Come, All Ye Faithful

Hark! The Herald Angels Sing

Winter

Vivaldi

The First Noel

Andante

Spring

Vivaldi

2

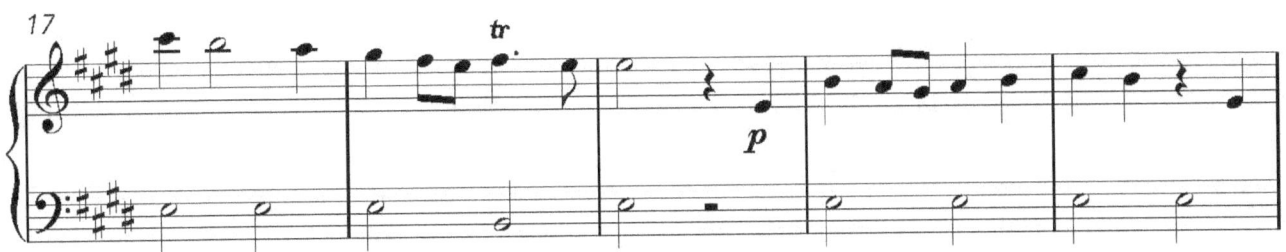

Menuet in G Major

Petzold

Pomp and Circumstance

Elgar

Bourée from Suite in E minor

Bach

Jesu, Joy of Man's Desiring

Bach

Gymnopédie No. 1

Satie

Adagio

2

Papageno's Aria No.1

Mozart

Allegro

2

Barcarolle

Offenbach

Moonlight Sonata

Beethoven

Difficult Pieces

American Patrol

2

Old King Cole

Andante

Air on the G String

Bach

Star Spangled Banner

2

Wedding March

Andante

Wagner

La Donna è Mobile

Verdi

2

Papageno's Aria No.2

Mozart

By the Light of the Silvery Moon

Joy to the World

Are You Lonesome Tonight?

2

O Holy Night

Too-Ra-Loo-Ra-Loo-Ral

2

Cavalleria Rusticana - Intermezzo

Mascagni

Adagio

Pathetique Sonata - 2nd Mov.

Beethoven

The Happy Farmer

Schumann

Étude in E Major

Chopin

2

Träumerei

Schumann

Piano Concerto No. 21 - 2nd Mov.

Mozart

2

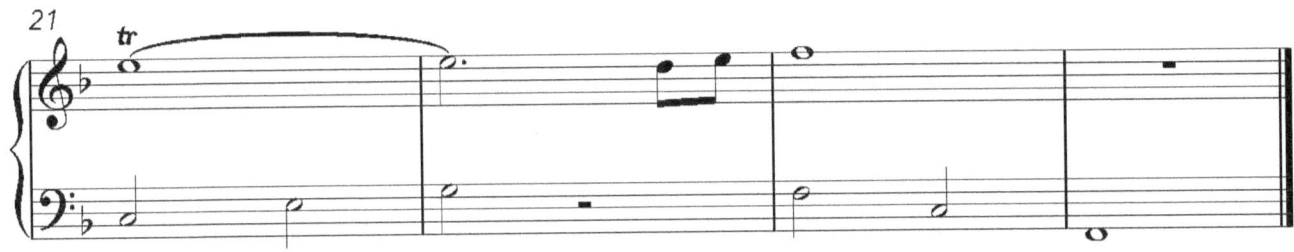

Very Difficult Pieces

Hello Ma Baby

Menuet in G Major

Bach

Andante

Beautiful Dreamer

The Entertainer

Take Me Out to the Ball Game

Allegro

The Blue Danube

Strauss

2

I'll See You in my Dreams

2

Down by the Riverside

Noctune in Eb Major

Chopin

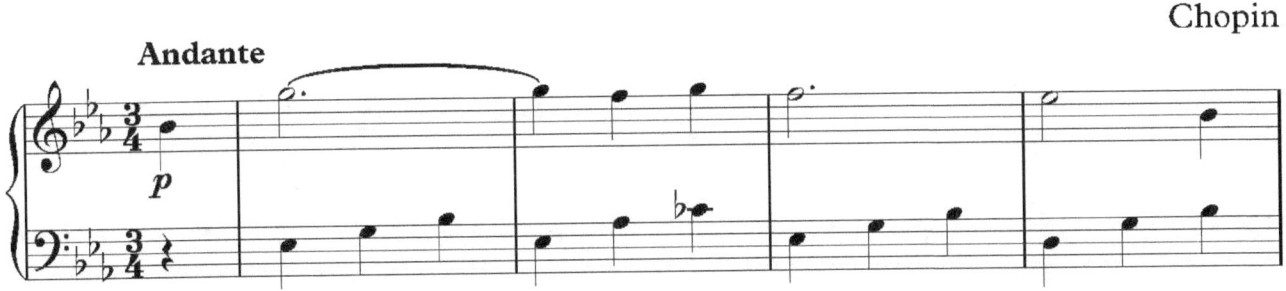

17

21

25

29

Menuet in A Major

Boccherini

Eine Kleine Nachtmusik

Mozart

2

Queen of the Night Aria

2

Für Elise

Beethoven

Andante

164

St. Louis Blues

O Sole Mio

Di Capua

2

Habanera

Bizet

Solace

Andante

Barber of Seville - Overture

Rossini

Allegro

It Had to be You

Conclusion

Thank you for joining us on this musical adventure with Piano Sheet Music for Beginners & Kids. As you journeyed through the pages of this book, we hope you found inspiration, joy, and fulfillment in the melodies that graced your piano keys. Whether you were captivated by the timeless classics of Mozart and Chopin, delighted by the charm of traditional folk tunes, or enchanted by the melodies of popular songs, your dedication to learning and exploring the world of piano playing is truly commendable.

As you continue to practice and refine your skills, remember that every note you play is a testament to your passion and commitment to music. Whether you're playing for your own enjoyment, sharing your talents with loved ones, or dreaming of larger stages, your journey as a pianist is a deeply personal and rewarding one.

We extend our heartfelt gratitude to you for choosing Piano Sheet Music for Beginners & Kids as your companion on your musical journey. May the melodies you've learned bring you endless hours of pleasure and serve as a reminder of the beauty and power of music in our lives.

Thanks for joining us on this adventure, and congratulations on completing this book of sheet music!

Happy playing!

Hey there, fellow music enthusiasts!

Now that you've enjoyed our delightful book, *Piano Sheet Music for Beginners & Kids*, we need your help to spread the joy and encourage others to join in on the harmonious fun! By leaving a review, you'll help aspiring pianists find the perfect guide and contribute to a world filled with more beautiful music. Here's a question: Have you ever considered how helping others can make a difference?

Leaving a review for *Piano Sheet Music for Beginners & Kids* is your chance to deliver value to others. By sharing your experience, insights, and thoughts, you can help potential musicians understand the true worth of this fantastic book. Whether you found it as an absolute game-changer in your or your child's musical journey or simply a delightful resource filled with engaging pieces, your review will guide others in their decision-making process.

Your review is crucial because countless beginners and young learners are searching for the perfect piano sheet music book but are overwhelmed by the vast selection available. Your words can shine a light on the brilliance of *Piano Sheet Music for Beginners & Kids* and give them the confidence to take the plunge. Imagine the smiles on their faces as they discover the joy of learning sheet music and the gratitude they'll feel toward you for sharing your thoughts!

So, here's our humble request: Please take a moment to leave an honest review for *Piano Sheet Music for Beginners & Kids* on your favorite online platform. Whether it's Amazon, Goodreads, or any other website where you purchased or discovered the book, your feedback matters immensely. It's super easy to do! Head to the book's page, scroll down to the review section, and let your fingers dance across the keyboard as you type your thoughts.

By leaving a review, you become part of a beautiful community of music lovers passionate about sharing their experiences. Your words can profoundly impact someone else's life, sparking a love for music that will last a lifetime. Isn't it amazing to think that a few minutes of your time can positively impact someone else's journey?

So, what are you waiting for? Grab your favorite device, hop onto your preferred online platform, and tell the world how *Piano Sheet Music for Beginners & Kids* has enriched your musical experience. Remember, your review can ignite a passion for piano in others and bring a symphony of joy to countless lives.

Thank you from the bottom of our musical hearts!

www.ingramcontent.com/pod-product-compliance
Lightning Source LLC
Chambersburg PA
CBHW080841120626
46553CB00009B/2521

* 9 7 9 8 9 8 8 9 9 3 8 1 0 *